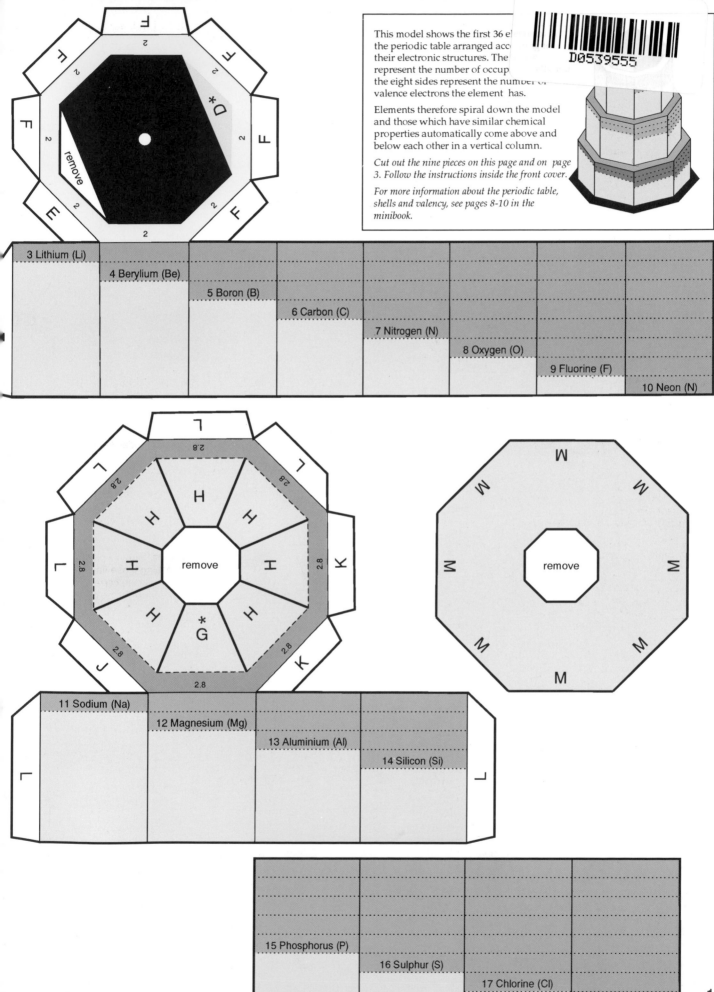

This model shows the first 36 el[...]
the periodic table arranged acc[...]
their electronic structures. The [...]
represent the number of occup[...]
the eight sides represent the number of
valence electrons the element has.

Elements therefore spiral down the model
and those which have similar chemical
properties automatically come above and
below each other in a vertical column.

*Cut out the nine pieces on this page and on page
3. Follow the instructions inside the front cover.*

*For more information about the periodic table,
shells and valency, see pages 8-10 in the
minibook.*

F F 2 D* F
remove
F 2 F 2
E 2 F 2

3 Lithium (Li)
4 Berylium (Be)
5 Boron (B)
6 Carbon (C)
7 Nitrogen (N)
8 Oxygen (O)
9 Fluorine (F)
10 Neon (N)

L 2.8
2.8 L
L 2.8 K
H H H
H remove H
H *G H
L 2.8 K
J 2.8
2.8

M M M
M M
remove
M M
M M
M

11 Sodium (Na)
12 Magnesium (Mg)
13 Aluminium (Al)
14 Silicon (Si)
L L

15 Phosphorus (P)
16 Sulphur (S)
17 Chlorine (Cl)
18 Argon (Ar)

                                                    C*   C

                                                          C

F   F   F   F   F   F   E

F
    H   H   H   H   H   G*   H

                                        M

                                    M   M

                        M   M

                            M   M
                                        M

                    K   K   J

                    O   O   N*   O

            L   L   L   L

    ⌐   ⌐
            O   O   O   O

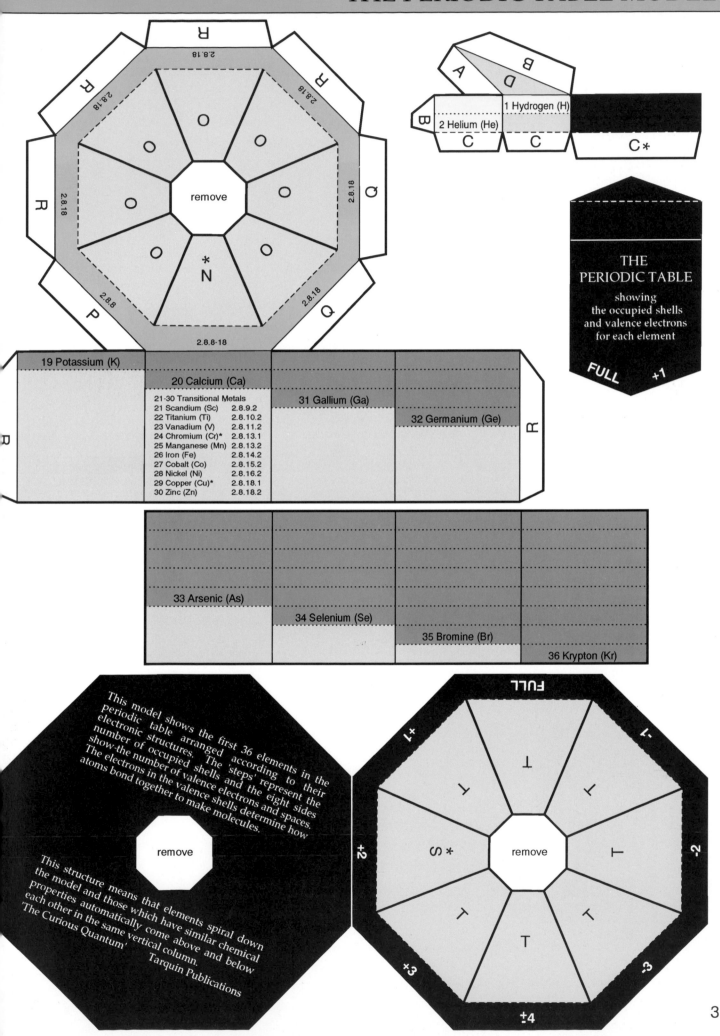

R
2.8.18
R
2.8.18
R
2.8.18
2.8.18
O O O O O O O O
remove
*N
2.8.18
R
Q
Q
2.8.8
P
2.8.8-18

A B
D
B
1 Hydrogen (H)
2 Helium (He)
C C C*

THE PERIODIC TABLE
showing the occupied shells and valence electrons for each element
FULL   +1

19 Potassium (K)

20 Calcium (Ca)

21-30 Transitional Metals
21 Scandium (Sc)   2.8.9.2
22 Titanium (Ti)   2.8.10.2
23 Vanadium (V)   2.8.11.2
24 Chromium (Cr)*   2.8.13.1
25 Manganese (Mn)   2.8.13.2
26 Iron (Fe)   2.8.14.2
27 Cobalt (Co)   2.8.15.2
28 Nickel (Ni)   2.8.16.2
29 Copper (Cu)*   2.8.18.1
30 Zinc (Zn)   2.8.18.2

31 Gallium (Ga)

32 Germanium (Ge)

R

33 Arsenic (As)

34 Selenium (Se)

35 Bromine (Br)

36 Krypton (Kr)

This model shows the first 36 elements in the periodic table arranged according to their electronic structures. The 'steps' represent the number of occupied shells and the eight sides show the number of valence electrons and spaces. The electrons in the valence shells determine how atoms bond together to make molecules.

remove

This structure means that elements spiral down the model and those which have similar chemical properties automatically come above and below each other in the same vertical column.
'The Curious Quantum'
Tarquin Publications

FULL
+1
-1
+2
S*
-2
remove
T T T T T T
+3
-3
±4

3

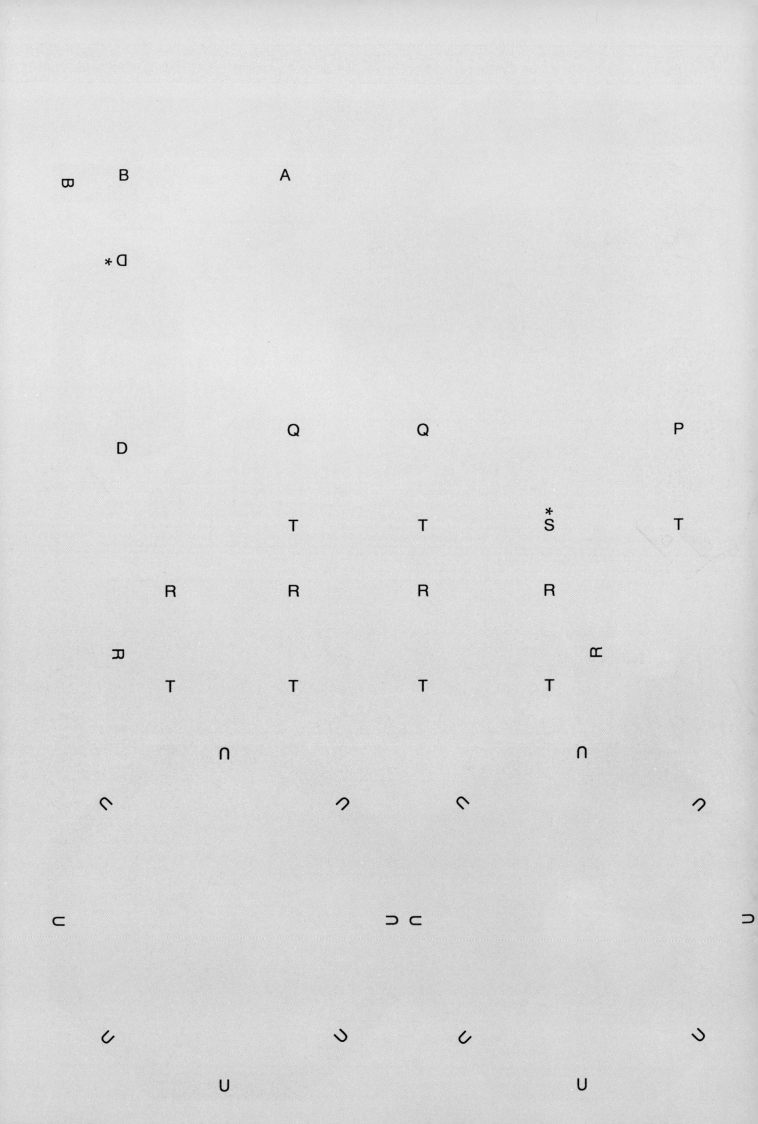

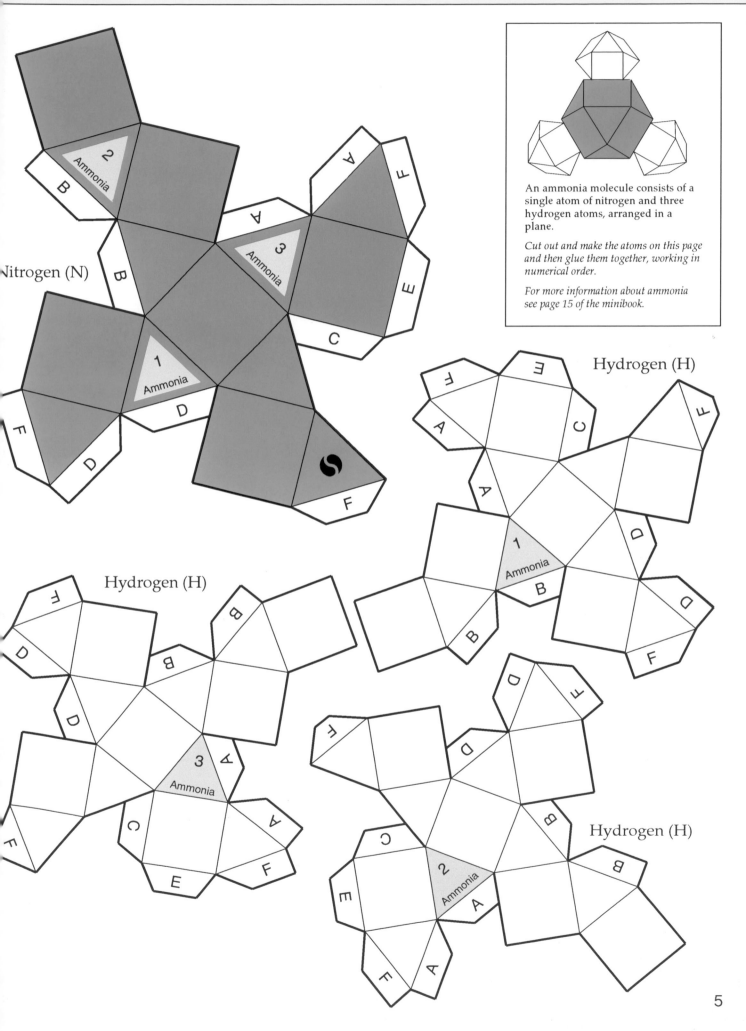

An ammonia molecule consists of a single atom of nitrogen and three hydrogen atoms, arranged in a plane.

Cut out and make the atoms on this page and then glue them together, working in numerical order.

For more information about ammonia see page 15 of the minibook.

Nitrogen (N)

Hydrogen (H)

Hydrogen (H)

Hydrogen (H)

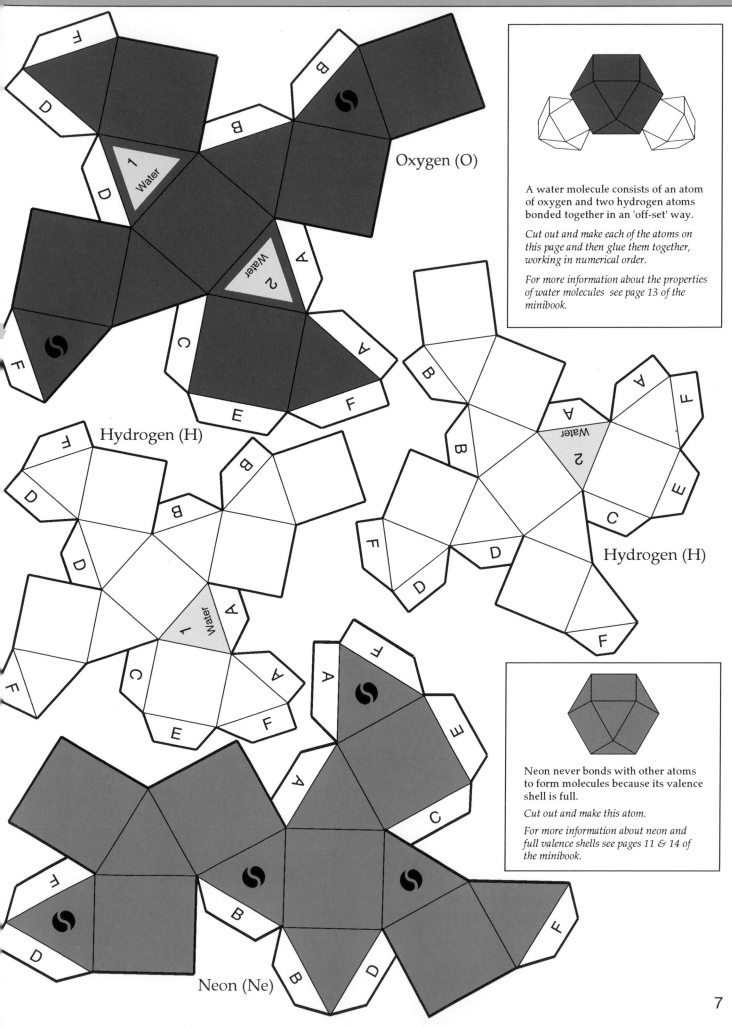

Oxygen (O)

Hydrogen (H)

Hydrogen (H)

Neon (Ne)

A water molecule consists of an atom of oxygen and two hydrogen atoms bonded together in an 'off-set' way.

Cut out and make each of the atoms on this page and then glue them together, working in numerical order.

For more information about the properties of water molecules see page 13 of the minibook.

Neon never bonds with other atoms to form molecules because its valence shell is full.

Cut out and make this atom.

For more information about neon and full valence shells see pages 11 & 14 of the minibook.

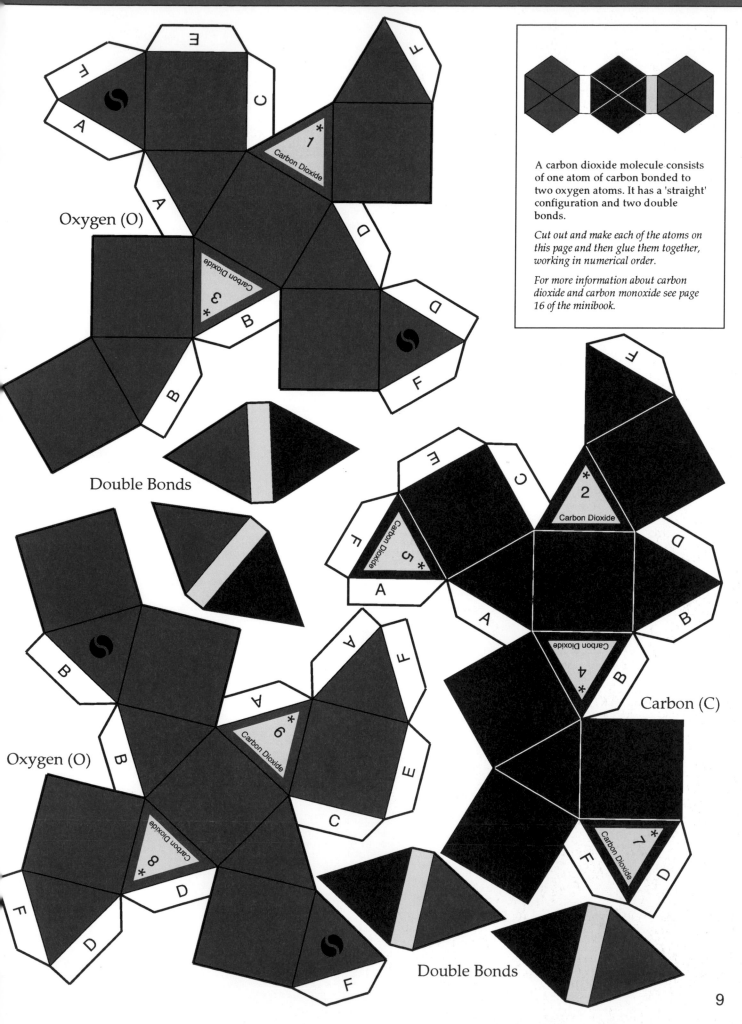

A carbon dioxide molecule consists of one atom of carbon bonded to two oxygen atoms. It has a 'straight' configuration and two double bonds.

Cut out and make each of the atoms on this page and then glue them together, working in numerical order.

For more information about carbon dioxide and carbon monoxide see page 16 of the minibook.

Oxygen (O)

Double Bonds

Carbon (C)

Oxygen (O)

Double Bonds

Carbon Dioxide

* 1
Carbon Dioxide

Carbon Dioxide
* 2

* 3
Carbon Dioxide

Carbon Dioxide
* 4

* 5
Carbon Dioxide

Carbon Dioxide
* 6

* 7
Carbon Dioxide

Carbon Dioxide
* 8

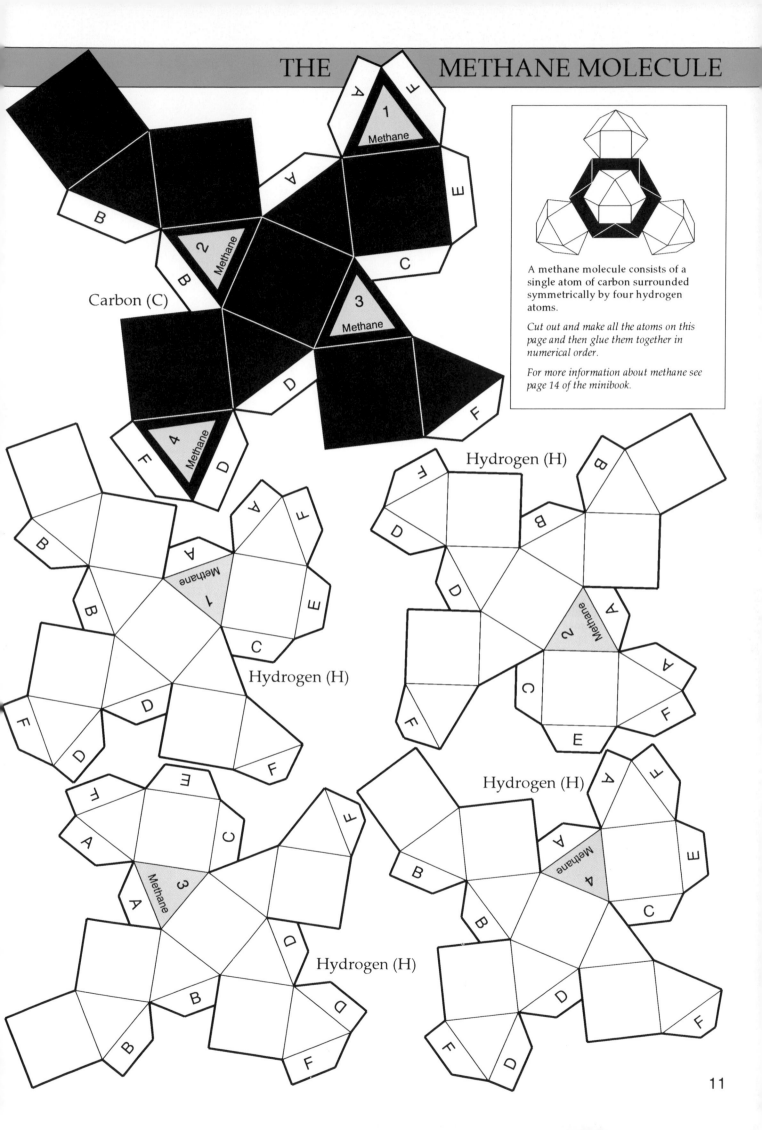

Carbon (C)

A methane molecule consists of a single atom of carbon surrounded symmetrically by four hydrogen atoms.

Cut out and make all the atoms on this page and then glue them together in numerical order.

For more information about methane see page 14 of the minibook.

Hydrogen (H)

Hydrogen (H)

Hydrogen (H)

Hydrogen (H)

THE
CURIOUS
QUANTUM

and its place in
fundamental chemistry

LEE BULBROOK

THE FIRST 36 ELEMENTS

ATOMIC NUMBER	ELEMENT	SYMBOL	APPROX ATOMIC WEIGHT	ATOMIC WEIGHT	ELECTRONIC STRUCTURE
1	Hydrogen	H	1.0	1.008	1,
2	Helium	He	4.0	4.003	2,
3	Lithium	Li	7.0	6.939	2, 1
4	Beryllium	Be	9.0	9.012	2, 2
5	Boron	B	11.0	10.81	2, 3
6	Carbon	C	12.0	12.01	2, 4
7	Nitrogen	N	14.0	14.01	2, 5
8	Oxygen	O	16.0	16.00	2, 6
9	Fluorine	F	19.0	19.00	2, 7
10	Neon	Ne	20.0	20.18	2, 8
11	Sodium	Na	23.0	22.99	2, 8, 1
12	Magnesium	Mg	24.0	24.31	2, 8, 2
13	Aluminium	Al	27.0	26.98	2, 8, 3
14	Silicon	Si	28.0	28.09	2, 8, 4
15	Phosphorus	P	31.0	30.99	2, 8, 5
16	Sulphur	S	32.0	32.06	2, 8, 6
17	Chlorine	Cl	35.5	35.45	2, 8, 7
18	Argon	Ar	40.0	39.95	2, 8, 8
19	Potassium	K	39.0	39.10	2, 8, 8, 1
20	Calcium	Ca	40.0	40.08	2, 8, 8, 2
21	Scandium	Sc	45.0	44.96	2, 8, 9, 2
22	Titanium	Ti	48.0	47.90	2, 8, 10, 2
23	Vanadium	V	51.0	50.94	2, 8, 11, 2
24	Chromium	Cr	52.0	52.00	2, 8, 13, 1
25	Manganese	Mn	55.0	54.94	2, 8, 13, 2
26	Iron	Fe	56.0	55.85	2, 8, 14, 2
27	Cobalt	Co	59.0	58.93	2, 8, 15, 2
28	Nickel	Ni	59.0	58.71	2, 8, 16, 2
29	Copper	Cu	63.5	63.54	2, 8, 18, 1
30	Zinc	Zn	65.0	65.37	2, 8, 18, 2
31	Gallium	Ga	70.0	69.72	2, 8, 18, 3
32	Germanium	Ge	72.5	72.59	2, 8, 18, 4
33	Arsenic	As	75.0	74.92	2, 8, 18, 5
34	Selenium	Se	79.0	78.960	2, 8, 18, 6
35	Bromine	Br	80.0	79.910	2, 8, 18, 7
36	Krypton	Kr	84.0	83.800	2, 8, 18, 8

0 906212 91 X
TARQUIN
PUBLICATIONS

We live in interesting times! Who would think that it could ever be possible to make simple paper models which are able to illustrate some of the most fundamental truths about the nature of the Universe?

By making models of a few simple molecules and considering why atoms bond together as they do, we can gain some insight into fundamental chemistry and acquire a certain understanding of the mysterious and curious quantum. The word itself comes from the Latin 'quantus' which means 'how much?', but this useful piece of information does not add very much to our understanding of its importance. Over recent years, the study of the quantum and the development of quantum mechanics have led to so many exciting discoveries in the field of fundamental science that we can now explain with ease chemical properties which were completely beyond the reach of even the most brilliant thinkers of the past.

Although it is not yet understood to any great extent by the general public, it is a fact that quantum mechanics is one of the most successful scientific theories ever. The difficulty is that it is normally expressed only in the form of difficult mathematical equations. However, with the aid of these models, this minibook and a little patience it is hoped that you will be able to appreciate to some extent what quantum mechanics is able to explain and what insights it is able to give us. Although the title of this book is 'The Curious Quantum', it is of course totally impossible to make a model of a quantum! However, it is possible to make sensible models of atoms, molecules and the periodic table and with them to see how essential the quantum is. Quantum mechanics can be thought of in much the same way as the glue which holds together your paper models. Without it, there would be no models. Without quantum mechanics there would be no satisfactory theory of atoms and molecules.

A QUESTION OF BALANCE

No-one can fail to wonder at the remarkable way in which living creatures are able to exploit chemical reactions. Without having to understand the curious quantum at all, they are able to make use of its consequences to further their own lives. When a magpie eats the body of a rabbit crushed by a car on a road, it is not aware that it is recycling nitrogen atoms which it is unable to extract from the air it uses to fly. Nor is it aware of the way it and other living systems have evolved to interact and complement each other and to make use of so many different molecules.

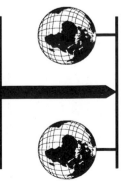

There is a theory, called the 'Gaia' theory, which suggests that all life on earth behaves as if it is part of a huge organism. All forms of life are acting in their own interests, but are dependent on all other forms in a complex interaction which makes the best use of the resources available. This Gaia, or whole earth interaction, is said to be responsible for the fact that life on earth has survived for billions of years in spite of enormous and catastrophic changes in circumstances.

However, that is another story.

For instance, a severe shock like the impact of a giant meteor 70 million years ago changed the climate sufficiently to cause the extinction of the dinosaurs. However, mammals then evolved rapidly to cope with the new circumstances and to make use of the foodstuffs which the disappearance of the dinosaurs made easily available. Life forms changed dramatically, but life on earth continued. An understanding of the Gaia mechanisms is of particular interest now when there are so many fears that man for the first time has the power to upset the balance catastrophically.

However, that is another story .....

QUARKS AND ALL THAT

It may seem strange to have reached the last page of a minibook about atoms and not to have mentioned the atomic bomb or radioactivity. The reason is a good one. As we have seen, fundamental chemistry is largely determined by the activity of electrons and electron shells and during chemical reactions the nucleus always remains unchanged. In contrast, in nuclear science it is the nucleus which is changed. The curious quantum is involved in the nucleus also and although chemistry can be explained very satisfactorily with protons, neutrons and electrons, the search for the ultimate 'indivisible particle' proposed by the Ancient Greeks is by no means over. The development of nuclear science and the building of giant accelerators able to smash particles into each other has led to the discovery of more and more distinct particles inside the atom. Some people believe that 'quarks' will be the end of the search, others are much more doubtful.

However, that is yet another story .....

If you have enjoyed this book then there may be other Tarquin titles which will interest you, in particular 'DNA -The Marvellous Molecule' by Borin Van Loon and 'The Chemical Helix' by Gerald Jenkins and Magdalen Bear. They are available from Bookshops, Toy Shops, Art/Craft Shops or in case of difficulty directly from Tarquin Publications, Stradbroke, Diss, Norfolk. IP21 5JP. England.

For an up-to-date catalogue of Tarquin books, please write to the publishers at the address above.

WHAT IS AN ATOM?

The word atom comes from the Greek word 'atomos' which means 'indivisible'. The Ancient Greeks loved to argue logically and to try to solve problems purely by thinking about them.

They said that if you took any quantity of a substance like wood, stone, water, salt, copper or bronze you could, in theory at least, divide it into two equal halves. They did not worry about the practical difficulties of doing this as Greek thinkers were seldom interested in practical experiments. They simply imagined that you could. Taking one of those halves, they argued that you could divide it into two halves again and choose one of them. This process could then be repeated and repeated, at each step getting a smaller quantity of the starting material. Common sense said that this process could not continue for ever, so eventually you would get down to a single particle of the substance.

This 'indivisible particle' was called the 'atom'.

The Greeks had no idea of how small it would be. At the time and for many years to follow, it was not appreciated that certain substances like copper, iron and sulphur, now called 'elements', were composed of atoms of only one kind whereas others like wood, stone, salt and water were compounds of atoms of several kinds. The word 'atom' is used only for the smallest particle of an element which does not lose its chemical nature. We now know that it is not an 'indivisible particle', but the name remains.

The smallest particle of a compound which does not lose its chemical nature is called a 'molecule' and how atoms bond together to make molecules is an important part of this book. Since atoms are more fundamental than molecules we shall concentrate on them first.

TINY BILLIARD BALLS

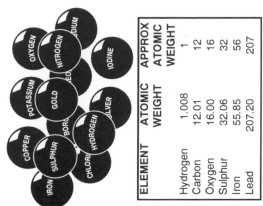

ELEMENT	ATOMIC WEIGHT	APPROX ATOMIC WEIGHT
Hydrogen	1.008	1
Carbon	12.01	12
Oxygen	16.00	16
Sulphur	32.06	32
Iron	55.85	56
Lead	207.20	207

As the centuries passed, it steadily became clearer which materials were elements and it was imagined that an atom of each separate element was a solid and distinct ball. As more and more elements were discovered, each was found to have a distinctive mass.

A single atom was far too small to weigh, but by a variety of methods it was possible to calculate the weight of one atom relative to another. Originally all 'atomic weights' were given in terms of hydrogen, the lightest element. For instance it was found that iron was about 56 times heavier and lead 207 times heavier than hydrogen. Later it was found to be more convenient to take the commonest form of carbon to be 12 precisely and to calculate every atomic weight relative to that.

What was the reason for so many atomic weights to be close to whole numbers and why is carbon listed here as 12.01 and not 12 precisely?

3

A QUESTION OF MOVEMENT AND SHAPE

Instructive as it is to make molecular models from cuboctahedron shapes, it is important to bear in mind that the bonds and interactions between real atoms are more flexible than a firmly glued model might suggest.

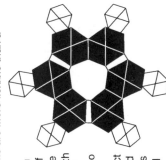

The benzene ring is a good example. It is made from 6 carbon and 6 hydrogen atoms arranged to form a hexagon. A count of the electrons and spaces show that each carbon atom must be joined to one neighbour with a single bond and to the other with a double bond. These conditions would be equally well met if the single and double bonds were to be interchanged. With two equally likely states, there is the possibility that the molecule could vibrate between the two states, as ammonia does. In fact it does not. The electrons distribute themselves equally around the ring in a flexible arrangement which has lower energy. This is one reason why the benzene ring is so resistant to chemical change.

When you built the cysteine model, you will no doubt have followed the markings in order to glue it together 'correctly'. Without those markings it is clear that it would have been possible to glue the same atoms into several different configurations, each satisfying all the requirements about full valence shells. Molecules adjust their shapes, attempting to reach the state of minimum energy in the circumstances they find themselves in. Certain units at the 'ends' of the molecule are free to rotate about their bonded neighbours. Their freedom of movement is not chaotic, but is limited by the presence of other 'ends' of molecules or indeed, other nearby molecules.

Making a model of a complex molecule is rather like trying to draw a picture of a moving animal. Although the limbs are joined to their bodies they can and do move about as much as the joints will allow. Different shapes of molecule with the same chemical make-up are called 'isomers'. All amino acids are isomers and this property allows the assembly of complex molecules of an almost infinite number of shapes. The word 'amino' refers to the nitrogen/hydrogen group and the connection with ammonia can be clearly seen. The term 'amine' is used to describe compounds obtained when the hydrogen atoms of ammonia are replaced with organic compounds. There are 20 different amino acids, but they all share a common structure. They have different 'side chains' giving them different characteristics and they can bond together in a multitude of orders with what is called a 'peptide bond'.

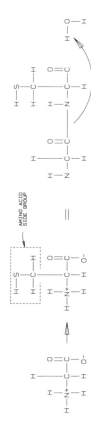

AMINO ACID SIDE GROUP

This illustration shows the forming of a peptide bond and the release of a molecule of water. The joint between any two amino acids is quite flexible and enables a string of molecules to twist and curl around each other to form complex shaped proteins. Ultimately, it is those atoms which find themselves on the outer surfaces of these complex molecules which determine how they react chemically and therefore what role they play in the living organism.

18

MENDELEYEV

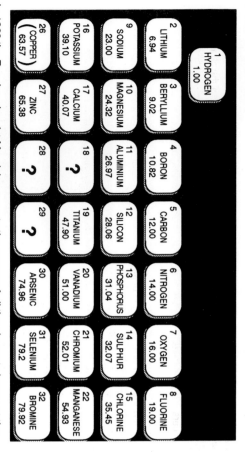

1 HYDROGEN 1.00							
2 LITHIUM 6.94	3 BERYLLIUM 9.02	4 BORON 10.82	5 CARBON 12.00	6 NITROGEN 14.00	7 OXYGEN 16.00	8 FLUORINE 19.00	
9 SODIUM 23.00	10 MAGNESIUM 24.32	11 ALUMINIUM 26.97	12 SILICON 28.06	13 PHOSPHORUS 31.04	14 SULPHUR 32.07	15 CHLORINE 35.45	
16 POTASSIUM 39.10	17 CALCIUM 40.07	18 ?	19 TITANIUM 47.90	20 VANADIUM 51.00	21 CHROMIUM 52.01	22 MANGANESE 54.93	
(26 COPPER 63.57	27 ZINC 65.38	28 ?	29 ?	30 ARSENIC 74.96	31 SELENIUM 79.2	32 BROMINE 79.92	

In 1869 the Russian chemist Mendeleyev wrote the names of all the elements known at the time on to separate cards and then arranged them into ascending order of atomic weight. He then set them out in a table in such a way that those elements which had similar chemical properties came one above the other. Others had tried this same approach and had failed, but he had the courage to leave gaps in his table, saying that there must be elements not yet discovered which would eventually fill them. He even forecast the properties they would have.

The illustration above shows part of Mendeleyev's table a year later, in 1870. Before long these new elements were indeed discovered and he was found to be substantially correct with his forecasts of their atomic weights and chemical properties. He called his table 'The Periodic Table' and it was of enormous importance. Everyone could see that if there were clear patterns of chemical connections between elements, then atoms could not be 'indivisible particles' and must have an internal structure. The race was on to find it.

A breakthrough came in 1897 when J.J.Thomson discovered a particle which had a mass only one 1840th of the mass of the hydrogen atom. It was negatively charged and was named the 'electron'. Soon afterwards it was discovered that electrons could be knocked out of atoms and there was great excitement in the scientific community. Atoms are electrically neutral, so if negative electrons could be knocked out then there must also be an equal number of positively charged particles in there too. These new positively-charged fundamental particles were called 'protons', meaning 'first' and were found to have a mass roughly equal to that of the hydrogen atom. It then became clear that a hydrogen atom consisted of just one proton and one electron.

It was also clear that many but not all differences between the atoms of different elements could be explained by the numbers of protons and electrons which they contained. There had to be a third kind of fundamental particle. One which had no charge and which had mass about the same as that of the proton. It was called the 'neutron' and it was finally identified in 1932.

The result of these discoveries was a wonderful simplification. For a while it seemed that every element in the universe was made out of just these three 'indivisible particles'.

| PROTONS |
| NEUTRONS |
| ELECTRONS |

CARBON - A VERY SPECIAL ELEMENT

It is estimated that there are about eleven million different kinds of molecule and that about ten million of them contain carbon atoms. It links with other atoms in more ways than any other element and has a special affinity with hydrogen, forming many different long chained and clustered molecules called hydrocarbons.

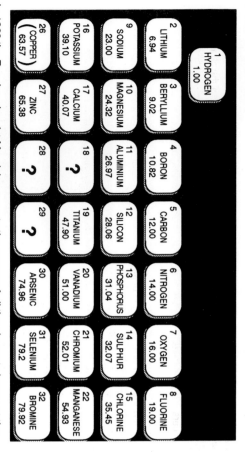

Methane, with one carbon and four hydrogen atoms can be regarded as the most basic hydrocarbon. However, if one hydrogen atom is removed from each of two methane atoms and their exposed carbons link, a new molecule called ethane is created. The chemical reactions which cause this to happen can be repeated, giving pentane and other similar molecules which are ingredients of petrols and fuel oils.

Carbon and hydrogen will also join together into relatively stable rings, called benzene rings. In their turn they will link together in many complex ways. Coal is an example of a substance which contains many benzene rings.

Man has learned to construct and manipulate carbon/hydrogen molecules to create great molecules which are of enormous use in modern life. Generally classified as synthetic materials, these substances include all the plastics like polythene, polypropylene, polyethylene etc. The very choice of the prefix 'poly', suggesting that a great many atoms are involved.

Methane

Ethane

Pentane

Benzene

CARBON BASED LIFE FORMS

With the addition of other elements, chiefly nitrogen and oxygen, carbon is a central building block of the molecules which make up living systems.

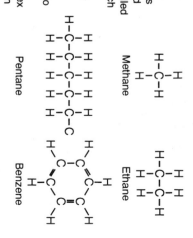

This illustration shows the model molecule of the amino acid cysteine. It consists of only fourteen atoms, but in common with other amino acids has the ability to link to many other molecules. Amino acids are the primary building blocks of larger molecules called proteins. Proteins may comprise solely of a chain of amino acids, but more frequently also combine with other structures such as fats and sugars. Some molecules essential to life, such as DNA, can contain millions of atoms bonded together into complex structures.

Science fiction writers, attempting to create life on remote planets have looked to other elements to serve as a basis for alien life-forms. Having looked at the periodic table for other elements with four valence electrons, their choices have fallen on silicon and germanium. It may be pure coincidence, but silicon and germanium are the materials used in computer chips and artificial intelligence systems. For the moment however, carbon based life forms reign supreme on earth!

WHAT ARE ISOTOPES?

It was discovered that although the number of protons in an atom is always the same as the number of electrons, the number of neutrons can vary. Neutrons do not affect the chemical properties of an element and so they do not feature very much in this book. However, they are an important part of the explanation of why the atomic weights of elements are not whole numbers. These different versions of an element with different numbers of neutrons were called 'isotopes' and any sample of an element contains different proportions or 'abundances' of them. Isotopes are named after the total number of 'nucleons' (protons and neutrons together) within the atom, so the commonest form of carbon is called 'Carbon 12'. Its atomic weight is 12 precisely, but a normal biological sample of carbon is made up of the three isotopes, Carbon 12, Carbon 13 and Carbon 14. The presence of the small quantites of the other heavier isotopes is enough to bring the average up to 12.01.

ISOTOPE	PROTONS	NEUTRONS	ELECTRONS	ABUNDANCE
Carbon 12	6	6	6	98.9%
Carbon 13	6	7	6	1.1%
Carbon 14	6	8	6	Trace

WHERE ARE THESE FUNDAMENTAL PARTICLES?

Having discovered that there were three kinds of fundamental particle inside the atom, many people thought they must be spread through it, rather like the fruit in a fruit cake. However modern scientists are very different from the Ancient Greek thinkers and they always want to test their theories and ideas by performing practical experiments. Cutting open a fruit cake to see what it looks like inside seems easy enough, but how could they see inside an atom? They searched for a method and learnt how to fire a stream of charged particles at and into atoms within a metal foil. The result was most surprising.

Most of the charged particles in the stream passed straight through the atoms and met with no obstacles at all. It was as if the atoms were not there. However, occasionally one of them bounced off in a most unexpected way, behaving just as if it had hit something really solid. Many repetitions quickly showed that almost all the mass of an atom was concentrated into an extremely small volume at its centre.

In an atom, all the protons and neutrons are gathered together into a minute 'nucleus', leaving a cloud of very light electrons to occupy the rest. Atoms are mostly empty space! The air of solidity that an atom normally has, is simply due to the 'everywhere and nowhere' property of its speeding electrons. It is rather similar to a busy motorway. There may be plenty of spaces between the speeding cars, but the overall effect is of a barrier which it is almost impossible to cross, at least at normal speeds.

The mental picture of an atom, showing a central dense nucleus surrounded by orbiting electrons is one that we all use, simply because it is such a convenient one. However, there are more difficulties with this idea than we might imagine.

THE CARBON DIOXIDE MOLECULE (CO₂)

$$\ddot{O} = C = \ddot{O}$$

The model shows that carbon dioxide is a 'straight' molecule. The carbon atom is equally spaced between the two oxygens and joined to each with a double bond. This arrangement completes the octet for each atom and with two double bonds, the gas is not easily reactive. Note how the double bonds are rotated through 90° relative to each other.

Carbon dioxide is a vital part in the chain of life as it is a molecule with a low total energy. Whenever it is formed, energy is released and becomes available for living processes to use. The energy required for you to read these words and to process their meaning in your brain is ultimately provided by the formation of carbon dioxide. It is the end point of the processes of breathing, burning, fermentation and all kinds of rotting and putrefaction.

Carbon dioxide is also emitted from some volcanoes and from certain springs of mineral water. There is a valley in Java and an area near mount Vesuvius in Italy where sufficient carbon dioxide seeps out of the ground to extinguish a flame. It is not a poisonous gas, but humans and animals suffocate if the level of concentration is too high. In direct contrast, plants are able to use the energy of sunlight to undo the double bonds and take the carbon for their own tissues. In doing this they release oxygen into the atmosphere. This balance between carbon dioxide and oxygen which is maintained by the interaction of plants and animals is associated with what is known as the 'Carbon Cycle'.

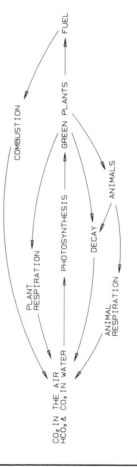

THE CARBON CYCLE

CARBON MONOXIDE (CO)

In this collection there is not a molecule of carbon monoxide to make but it is similar in shape to the nitrogen molecule, being one atom of carbon and one atom of oxygen joined by a triple bond. Carbon monoxide has some similar properties to nitrogen, but the triple bond is less stable because the octets are not complete and can be broken more easily. It is often formed when a source of carbon burns in the absence of sufficient oxygen. Unlike carbon dioxide, it is a very poisonous gas because it has no smell and combines very readily with the haemoglobin in blood, in fact about 200 times more readily than oxygen molecules do. It forms stable molecules called carboxy-haemoglobin which will not give up the carbon monoxide or allow the release of oxygen into the body. Since the oxygen supply is halted, this causes a rapid reduction in vital activity and then death.

WHAT IS THE PROBLEM?

It was soon appreciated that negative electrons do remain outside the positive nucleus, although no-one could explain how they could do so.

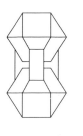

Because of the force of attraction between positive and negative charges, if an electron were ever to become stationary in the neighbourhood of the nucleus, then it would be attracted inwards and would attach itself to the nucleus. This does not happen, and people remembered that it was the orbital motion which prevented this. Perhaps electrons might orbit the nucleus in a similar way?

Of course, in the case of electrons, it is charge which is important, not gravity, but the effect would be the same. However, there is an important additional point to consider. If a negative electron were to orbit around a positive nucleus then it should behave like a minute transmitter and radiate electromagnetic energy outwards. As it loses this energy the electron would be expected to spiral inwards and disappear into the nucleus in a fraction of a second. Plainly, it does not!

Electrons cannot orbit, but they do!
They should fall into the nucleus, but they don't!

ENTER QUANTUM MECHANICS!

Explaining this paradox caused a great deal of rethinking and puzzling, with the result that a startling discovery was made. It can be summarised as:

Energy only exists in packets.

The word quantum with its plural quanta was the name chosen for these minute fundamental packets of energy. It may not seem to be a very important or revolutionary idea, but it is the equivalent of saying that a car can only travel at speeds 10mph, 20mph, or 30mph, but at no speeds in between. It must instantaneously jump from one speed to the other and not accelerate between them.

Common sense tells us that this idea must be wrong but in this case it misleads us. Speeds really do increase in a series of jumps, but the jumps are so small that we cannot detect them any more than we can detect the atoms in the steering wheel of the same car. Common sense does not inform us that the atoms in the head of a hammer or of a nail are mostly empty space, yet most people do not have problems in accepting that this is the truth. Quanta become easier when we get used to them! The expression 'a quantum leap' has already entered ordinary speech, but without any idea of just how small a real 'quantum leap' is.

Energy can only be added or lost one quantum at a time and this is very important indeed on the scale of atoms and molecules. An electron in an atom cannot spiral inwards towards the nucleus, losing energy gradually. It must jump instantaneously from one orbit to another and lose exactly one quantum in the process. Although this explanation indicated that orbits must be arranged in 'steps' of some kind, it was not obvious whether or not there would be a 'lowest step'. However it was proved that there had to be one and eventually the solution to the mystery was found in the form of a mathematical equation, the Schrödinger equation.

$$-\frac{\hbar^2}{2m}\nabla^2\psi + V(r)\psi = E\psi$$

THE AMMONIA MOLECULE (NH₃)

Nitrogen has five electrons in its outer shell. It therefore needs only three hydrogen atoms to complete its octet. These hydrogen atoms lie in a ring in a plane with the nitrogen atom offset to one side. Inspection of the model will quickly show that the nitrogen atom could just as well have been on the other side of the hydrogen ring. In fact, the nitrogen atom 'pops' backwards and forwards through the ring and between these two possible states. This vibrating characteristic of the ammonia atom was used in one of the earlier atomic clocks.

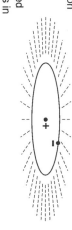

H
|
H—N—H
∴

In the methane molecule the four hydrogens give true tetrahedral symmetry. In ammonia however, the symmetry is little broken because the remaining unshared electrons form a lone-pair. Lone-pairs repel shared orbitals a little more strongly than shared orbitals repel each other and they therefore force the hydrogen atoms a little closer together than the model shows. In fact the real angle should be 107.3° and not the 109.5° given by the tetrahedral arrangement of the model.

THE NITROGEN MOLECULE (N₂)

This model is a simple one to make, but it is an important one. It shows how two nitrogen atoms bond together to form a nitrogen molecule. Each atom has to fill three spaces in its outer shell to complete its octet. They do this by sharing three electrons. This kind of sharing is known as a "triple bond" and it is the strongest way for any two atoms to join together. As a result, nitrogen in the atmosphere behaves almost as if it were an inert gas.

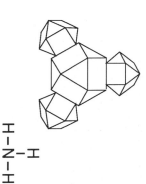

:N≡N:

Although 78% of the air we breathe is in the form of nitrogen molecules, they are so inert that we are quite unable to use them to supply our bodily needs of nitrogen. Our DNA contains it, as do the proteins and amino acids essential for our survival. All the nitrogen which we need to live and grow has to come to us in a form where the triple bonds have already been undone. We have to obtain all of it from the plants and animal products which we eat as food. However, neither plants nor animals are able to use the triple bonded nitrogen in the atmosphere either. Fortunately there are some 'nitrogen fixing' bacteria in the soil which can undo the triple bonds. Another important source of nitrogen for living things is from electrical discharges in thunderstorms. They cause the nitrogen to combine with oxygen and make nitrogenous salts. Rain then washes them into the soil, where they are taken up by the roots of plants and used to form their nucleic acids and proteins. Animals then eat the plants and make use of these proteins. In turn some nitrogen is then returned to the soil in their waste products and further bacteria in the soil reconvert these simple nitrogen compounds into forms which plants can re-use. This complete process is known as the 'Nitrogen Cycle'.

Another indication of how reactive nitrogen is when it is not triple bonded comes from its importance in explosives. Nitro-glycerine and TNT are examples of nitrogen compounds which react explosively when stimulated by heat or shock.

ORBITS AND ORBITALS

The Schrödinger equation is a partial differential equation which is easy to write down, but difficult to solve. It only has an exact solution for hydrogen, the simplest atom of all and for a few other simple cases, but the use of powerful computers now allows us to obtain solutions to the equation for other atoms and also for many molecules. In ordinary school algebra, we expect equations to have just one or two solutions. However, this equation has an infinite series of solutions, each corresponding to a possible orbit.

At this stage we must abandon the idea that an electron orbiting the nucleus is at all like the earth orbiting the sun. In fact, we must abandon the use of the word 'orbit' itself because it suggests a clear, precise path which the electron could take. Instead we use the word 'orbital' to describe a region of space where the electron might be found.

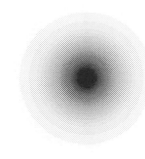

A solution of the Schrödinger equation does not tell us exactly where an electron is, but gives the probability of finding the electron in each region of the orbital. That is why it is known as a 'probability statement' and why it is customary to represent an orbital by a fuzzy diagram. The darker the shading, the more likely it is that the electron will be found there. Of course, this diagram is only a representation of the three-dimensional orbital!

PROBABILITIES IN ORBITALS

It can be helpful to try to understand orbitals by thinking of an electron orbiting the nucleus many billions of times each second. According to its probability statement the electron visits regions of the orbital frequently or rarely. The higher the probability associated with a particular location the more likely the electron is to be found there. We could also say that it spends more time in regions where the probability is high and less time in regions where the probability is low. You might well ask how the electron 'knows' where it is to go next and that is a very good question.

The answer lies in the nature of the electron itself. Just as the orbital seems to dissolve into fuzziness, so does the electron. An electron does seem to be a particle if you observe it from a distance or are concerned about directing a stream of electrons at a screen in a TV set or a computer monitor. However the more closely you examine it, the more strange and vague it becomes. It is a curious fact that J.J.Thomson received a Nobel Prize for proving that an electron was a particle and his son, G.P.Thomson, received one for proving that it was a wave! This dual wave-particle nature of matter is established beyond doubt when an electron is outside the atom. Within it, its nature is even more mysterious. Electrons and their orbitals can really only be described in mathematical terms and so any mental pictures we have or diagrams we can draw are only useful as convenient approximations. We use them throughout this book, but it is essential to maintain a healthy scepticism of them all.

However, do not imagine that because the diagrams and our descriptions seem to be rather vague that there is anything vague about the results one can calculate. Quantum mechanics does allow us to explain the properties of atoms and molecules brilliantly.

For instance, let us now consider the idea of 'energy levels'.

THE NEON ATOM (Ne)

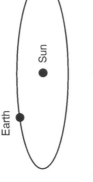

The simplest model to make is one of the noble gases and neon is a typical example. The model shows how the four lone pairs of electrons in a full valence shell take up the tetrahedral symmetry shown in the tetrahedron model. The noble gases, helium, neon, argon, krypton, xenon and radon do not join together to make molecules but exist almost without exception in atomic form only. It is because the outer shell is filled so symmetrically and shields the positive nucleus, that there is little tendency for them to bond at all.

For many years it was believed that there were no compounds of any of these elements, but recently some compounds of fluorine with krypton and xenon have been found. No compounds of helium, argon or neon have yet been discovered, but it would be foolhardy to say that they are absolutely impossible.

THE METHANE MOLECULE (CH$_4$)

This model shows the tetrahedral symmetry of a full valence shell and it does so because the four electrons which carbon needs to share to complete its octet are provided by four hydrogen atoms. Each of the hydrogen atoms also completes its duet and conditions for a stable molecule are met. It might remind us of the electron symmetry of the inert gases, but methane combines readily with oxygen and serves as an excellent fuel. It burns with a clean blue flame to give carbon dioxide, water and lots of heat.

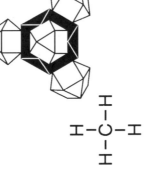

Methane is the main component of natural gas and is produced by bacteria from rotting vegetation. The huge reserves of natural gas found trapped in rocks in many parts of the world were produced millions of years ago, but the process also continues today. It can be seen to bubble out of marshes and damp ground mixed with carbon dioxide and is occasionally known to self-ignite to give a ghostly blue will-o'-the-wisp flickering like a over marshes on a still night.

Coal is also a product of ancient vegetation and methane associated with it often seeps into the galleries and shafts of mines. In mines it is known as 'fire damp' and in certain concentrations can explode violently when ignited by the slightest flame or spark.

A less explosive, but still significant source of methane in the atmosphere is from the digestive tracts of ruminant animals like cattle. In recent times there has been a dramatic increase in the number of cattle worldwide and since methane is an important 'greenhouse effect' gas, it is thought possible that this could contribute to a change in the climate.

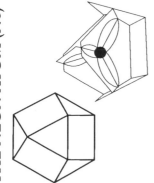

ENERGY LEVELS

This diagram shows a side view of some ordinary steps leading up from horizontal ground. It can serve as a useful model of the idea of energy levels within atoms and molecules.

Let us imagine that someone has placed an apple on each of the three lowest steps and that these apples are identical. The energy that we are talking about in this example is called 'potential energy' or 'gravitational energy'. We can say that each horizontal tread represents a stable energy level, a place where an apple can remain until disturbed by some external force or event.

It can be said that each of the three apples occupies a different energy level and it makes sense to number the steps 1,2,3... starting with the lowest. To raise an apple to a higher step requires work against the force of gravity and this work raises it to a higher energy level. Similarly an apple falling to a lower step would release energy and this energy would appear in the form of motion. The lowest apple is on the ground and cannot fall lower.

We also talk of energy levels being 'occupied' or 'vacant'. In the example above we can say that the three lower energy levels 1,2,3 are occupied and the three higher energy levels 4,5,6 are vacant.

ELECTRON SHELLS

Within atoms there are energy levels, although not because of gravity but because the negative electrons are close to a positive nucleus. The 'steps' idea can help us to understand energy levels but in an atom they have to be regarded as three-dimensional 'shells' surrounding the nucleus. Within each shell there are one or more orbitals in which an electron can be found and the 'steps' between the shells are unequal in size. The lowest energy level in an atom is known as the 'ground state' and the ideas of quantum mechanics demand that there is one. Classical physics did not and this was a strong reason why it had to be abandoned and replaced with quantum theory.

Bringing all these ideas together, the number of orbitals generates a remarkable pattern.

Shell 1 (ground state)	1	=	1 orbital
Shell 2	1 + 3	=	4 orbitals
Shell 3	1 + 3 + 5	=	9 orbitals
Shell 4	1 + 3 + 5 + 7	=	16 orbitals
Shell 5	and so on		

It can be seen that the number of orbitals in each shell is the square of the shell number. It might be thought that in multi-electron atoms, just one electron would occupy each possible orbital, and that those orbitals with the lowest energy would be the first to be occupied. However quantum mechanics has another surprise to offer, the idea of electron 'spin'.

THE WATER MOLECULE (H$_2$O)

Water covers approximately seven tenths of the surface of the earth and there are great masses of it in the atmosphere. This tiny molecule truly dominates life on earth and we ourselves are mostly water. It is a vital part of almost all living processes.

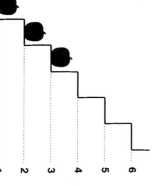

That water is a liquid at normal temperatures is something of an oddity for such a small molecule. This is largely due to its offset shape. An electron being shared between the oxygen and a hydrogen, tends to spend most of its time between the two nuclei. This exposes the positive charge of the hydrogen nucleus. Hence there is more positive charge on the side with the hydrogens and more negative charge on the side of the oxygen. Molecules which are unevenly charged like this are said to be 'polar'.

This polar effect is not a very strong force, but it causes the water molecules to tend to hold together. The positive side of one molecule attracts the negative side of others. This attractive force is called a 'hydrogen bond', but really it could have been called a 'charge bond' or an 'electrostatic bond'. At room temperatures these bonds are constantly being broken and reformed and the water remains a liquid. Only when the temperature is raised above 100°C does the jostling become too severe for the hydrogen bonds to restrain the molecules and the liquid water becomes gaseous steam.

Water molecules do allow light to pass through them but the hydrogen bonds absorb some red photons, letting through photons with longer wavelengths. This explains the blue tinge of deep water or thick ice. Water also has a curious property as it cools into its solid form (ice). As the temperature falls towards 0°C and it begins to freeze, the breaking and reforming of the hydrogen bonds slows and a regular hexagonal structure establishes itself.

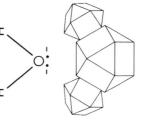

This hexagonal structure is at the molecular level and far, far smaller than a snowflake. However, it is thought that this explains the six-sided symmetry and almost infinite variety of snowflakes. They grow step by step, molecule by molecule and preserve this underlying symmetry. The most impressive snowflakes form at between -12°C and -16°C.

The crystalline structure of ice is less dense than liquid water and therefore ice forms on the surface and does not sink to the bottom. This surface layer of ice also acts as a good insulator, greatly slowing the rate at which the water below loses heat and freezes. Water is at its densest at 4°C and even in the harshest winter, the bottom layers of ponds, rivers and the sea seldom fall below that temperature or freeze right to the bottom.

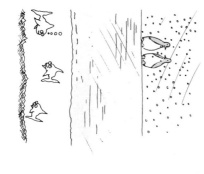

This property of the water molecule is thought to have played a vital role in the evolution of life on earth by allowing aquatic life to survive through the winter.

ELECTRON SPIN

In the early days, electrons were imagined to be minute globes. From this idea it seemed a small step to the notion that they might be spinning about an axis. This suggestion seemed to explain certain features about the behaviour of atoms and molecules. A globe can spin one way or the other but how we describe it depends where we are looking from.

Look at it this way and the spin is clockwise

Look at it this way and the spin is anticlockwise

The diagram above shows that there can only be two 'states' of spin which we can call clockwise and anticlockwise or positive and negative and an electron must have either one or the other. Anything which spins has angular momentum, and this quantity also exists only in packets or quanta. Usually they are called '+1/2' and '-1/2'. Modern ideas say that an electron is not a minute globe and it is not really spinning, but 'spin' is an attribute of matter just as 'charge' or 'mass' is. Although we cannot really describe what spin is, except mathematically, it is convenient to continue to use the mental image, as long as we do not think of it too literally. To emphasise this point, there are other particles which are not mentioned in this book because they do not play a part in chemistry, which have 3 or 4 states of spin.

When we come to consider the orbitals of atoms other than hydrogen, the spin of an electron becomes very important.

CHARGE AND EXCLUSION

The hydrogen atom has only a single electron and we can imagine it flitting from orbital to orbital as it gains and loses energy one quantum at a time. In other atoms where there are two or more electrons, the behaviour of the electrons is influenced by the fact that they are negatively charged and therefore repel each other. Because of these repulsions it might be expected that never more than one electron would ever be found in the same orbital. This is partially true but there is one very important exception. Two electrons can share an orbital if their spins are different. There is a law of nature which says:

Electrons with opposite spins will share an orbital as long as all the other orbitals at that energy level are occupied.

This law is also a consequence of what is called the 'Pauli Exclusion Principle'. The table opposite can be modified to give:

Shell 1 (ground state)	1	= 1 orbital	maximum of 2 electrons
Shell 2	1 + 3	= 4 orbitals	maximum of 8 electrons
Shell 3	1 + 3 + 5	= 9 orbitals	maximum of 18 electrons
Shell 4	1 + 3 + 5 + 7	= 16 orbitals	maximum of 32 electrons
Shell 5	and so on		

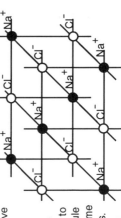

When two electrons with opposite spins do share an orbital then they are called a "lone pair". On the models this symbol is used to represent them.

Remember that although it is convenient to talk of electron shells, it must not be thought that in reality they are rigidly separated from each other. However, since chemical properties are largely determined by the electrons in the outer shell, known as the 'valence shell', we can safely concentrate on them and ignore what happens to the others in the inner shells.

9

COVALENT BONDS

Let us start with the simplest molecule of all, the hydrogen molecule. When two hydrogen atoms bond together, they each provide one electron. This 'duet' of shared electrons satisfies the Lewis rule that each atom 'wishes' to complete its valence shell. In the case of the inner shell, two electrons are enough. This diagram shows that both electrons are most likely to be found in the region between the two nuclei. This negatively charged region attracts both positively charged protons inwards and serves as a kind of glue which holds the molecule together.

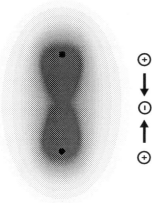

Bonds where two atoms share a single electron are known as single bonds. Other pairs of atoms can share either two electrons (double bond) or three electrons (triple bond).

Water
Single bonds

Carbon Dioxide
Double bonds

Nitrogen
Triple bond

$$(+) \longrightarrow (-) \longleftarrow (+)$$

IONIC BONDS

Sometimes another kind of bonding takes place, called 'ionic bonding' and sodium chloride (common salt) is a convenient example to use. The Lewis rule says that atoms other than hydrogen are 'looking for' electrons to complete an octet in the valence shell. Chlorine already has seven valence electrons and is 'looking for' one more. In some circumstances it does not just share an electron with another atom, but borrows it permanently and incorporates it into its own shell. The result is not a new element, because the number of protons is unchanged, but an ion. A chlorine ion has 17 protons and 18 electrons and so is negatively charged. Similarly a sodium atom has only one electron in its valence shell and is 'willing' to lose it to the chlorine, leaving a completed shell exposed. The result is a sodium ion with 11 protons and 10 electrons which is positively charged.

These positive and negative ions are attracted to one another, but not simply one to one. Six positive ions cluster around each negative ion and six negative ions cluster around each positive ion.

The result is a giant cubical lattice, the crystalline substance we call common salt. It is not sensible to make a model of a single sodium chloride molecule because it cannot really be said to exist in the same way as a single covalently bonded molecule does.

All the models in this book are covalently bonded.

12

VALENCY AND THE PERIODIC TABLE

It is a consequence of quantum mechanics, orbitals and energy levels that the inner shell can only hold a maximum of 2 electrons. Further electrons then begin to occupy shells 2,3,4,5 etc. with their maximum numbers of 8, 18, 32, 50 etc., but another restriction also comes into play.

The valence shell must contain at least 1 and never more than 8 electrons.

We are now able to explain very successfully the underlying reason for those periodic connections between elements which Mendeleyev noticed so long ago.

Elements in the same chemical group have the same number of valence electrons.

	GROUP 1		
3	Lithium	Li	2, 1
11	Sodium	Na	2, 8, 1
19	Potassium	K	2, 8, 8, 1
37	Rubidium	Rb	2, 8, 18, 8, 1
55	Caesium	Cs	2, 8, 18, 18, 8, 1

	GROUP 7		
9	Fluorine	F	2, 7
17	Chlorine	Cl	2, 8, 7
35	Bromine	Br	2, 8, 18, 7
53	Iodine	I	2, 8, 18, 18, 7
85	Astatine	At	2, 8, 18, 32, 18, 7

Mendeleyev was not aware of the existence of the noble gases. They are so unreactive that during his lifetime they had not been identified at all. You will see that none of them was included in the illustration on page 4. However, once they were discovered, it was a simple matter to add an extra vertical column to the periodic table and to call it group 0.

	GROUP 0		
2	Helium	He	2,
10	Neon	Ne	2, 8,
18	Argon	Ar	2, 8, 8,
36	Krypton	Kr	2, 8, 18, 8
54	Xenon	Xe	2, 8, 18, 18, 8
86	Radon	Rn	2, 8, 18, 32, 18, 8

The essential point about all these inert elements is that their outer shells are full. It is called group 0 because there is no space for further electrons in that shell.

THE PERIODIC TABLE MODEL

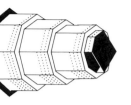

This model is able to show important features of the structure of atoms including the shell structure. Whenever there are electrons in a new shell, there is a step and the diameter of the model increases. This means that all elements with the same number of occupied shells come together on the same section of the model. Because the model has eight sides, corresponding to the possible numbers of valence electrons, those elements which have similar chemical properties automatically come above and below each other in the same vertical column. The elements spiral down the model as the atomic number increases.

Note how the ten 'transitional metals', elements 21-30 have been placed on the model. Once there are two electrons in the valence shell, the additional electrons go into the third shell until the number there reaches the maximum possible of 18. It will also be observed that Chromium and Copper are slight exceptions. They have only one valence electron and the other drops down into the third shell. Detailed calculations show that this arrangement has a very slightly lower energy level.

TETRAHEDRAL SYMMETRY

The noble gases are the only elements with full valence shells and they have such stability and resistance to taking part in chemical reactions that it is instructive to see how their electrons are arranged.

The tetrahedron model is able to do this. It shows what happens when there is an 'octet' of eight electrons in the valence shell. We know that only four orbitals are available, so the electrons must be arranged into pairs with opposite spins. These lone-pairs repel each other equally and so they naturally settle into the symmetrical tetrahedral arrangement shown on this model.

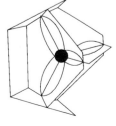

MOLECULES AND THE LEWIS RULE

The atoms of elements other than the noble gases do not have a complete octet of electrons in the outer shell and therefore their electrons do not arrange themselves into such a symmetrical, low-energy configuration. They are therefore able to react with other atoms and join together to make molecules.

The American chemist Gilbert Lewis pointed out that when atoms do bond together to form molecules they behave as if they 'wish' to complete an octet in the outer valence shell by sharing electrons with other atoms. Although it seems more vivid and personal to think of atoms 'wishing' something, remember that it is really a search for the configuration with the lowest possible energy. The Lewis rule can be stated as:

A molecule forms when all the atoms in it succeed in sharing electrons to complete their octets.

The exception to this rule is hydrogen because shell 1 only needs two electrons to be complete. An 'octet' for hydrogen is therefore a 'duet'!

The geometrical shape used for the atomic models in this book is called a 'cuboctahedron'. It is obtained from a cube by slicing off all eight corners. The reason why this shape works so well for the model molecules is because it is able to mimic the 'completing an octet' property of bonding atoms required by the Lewis rule.

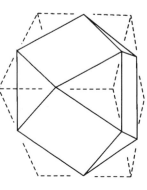

It is able to represent the eight electrons and the four orbitals in their preferred tetrahedral arrangement. Model 'atoms' made by glueing these model 'atoms' together are therefore realistic representations of the true shapes of real molecules.

Atoms are bounded by their whirling electrons and their sizes depend to some extent by the company they are keeping and the bonds they are making. It would be misleading to try to show the relative sizes of atoms by fine-tuning the sizes of the models, so this has been done only in the crudest possible way. The smallest model is hydrogen because it is the smallest atom. The models of atoms with electrons in two shells, carbon, oxygen and nitrogen have been made equal and a little larger. Sulphur, with electrons in three shells has been made a little larger still.

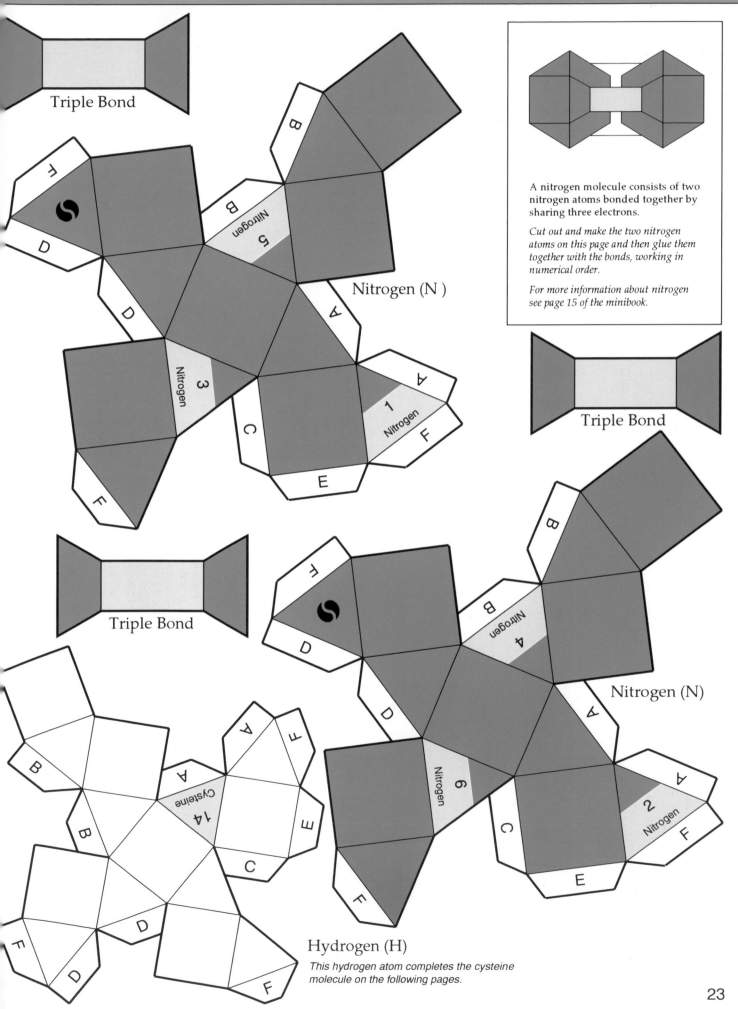

Triple Bond

Nitrogen (N)

5 Nitrogen

3 Nitrogen

1 Nitrogen

A nitrogen molecule consists of two nitrogen atoms bonded together by sharing three electrons.

Cut out and make the two nitrogen atoms on this page and then glue them together with the bonds, working in numerical order.

For more information about nitrogen see page 15 of the minibook.

Triple Bond

Triple Bond

4 Nitrogen

Nitrogen (N)

6 Nitrogen

2 Nitrogen

14 Cysteine

Hydrogen (H)

This hydrogen atom completes the cysteine molecule on the following pages.

23

Nitrogen

1

Nitrogen

2

Nitrogen

3

Nitrogen

4

Nitrogen

5

Nitrogen

6

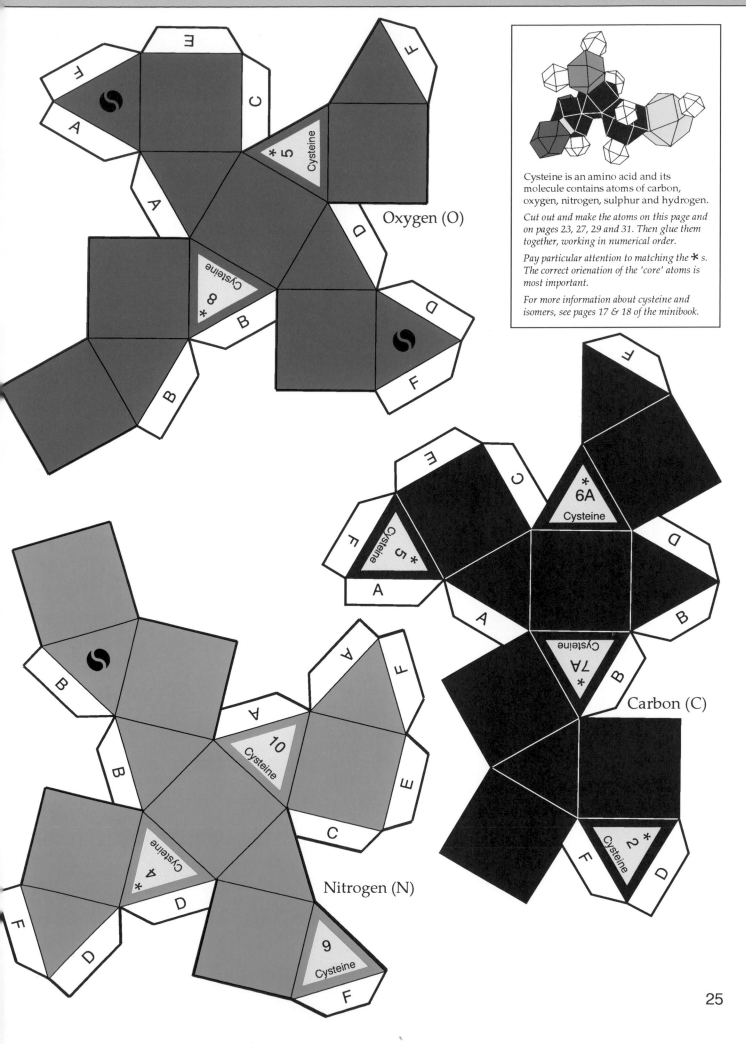

Cysteine is an amino acid and its molecule contains atoms of carbon, oxygen, nitrogen, sulphur and hydrogen.

Cut out and make the atoms on this page and on pages 23, 27, 29 and 31. Then glue them together, working in numerical order.

Pay particular attention to matching the ✱ s. The correct orienation of the 'core' atoms is most important.

For more information about cysteine and isomers, see pages 17 & 18 of the minibook.

Oxygen (O)

Carbon (C)

Nitrogen (N)

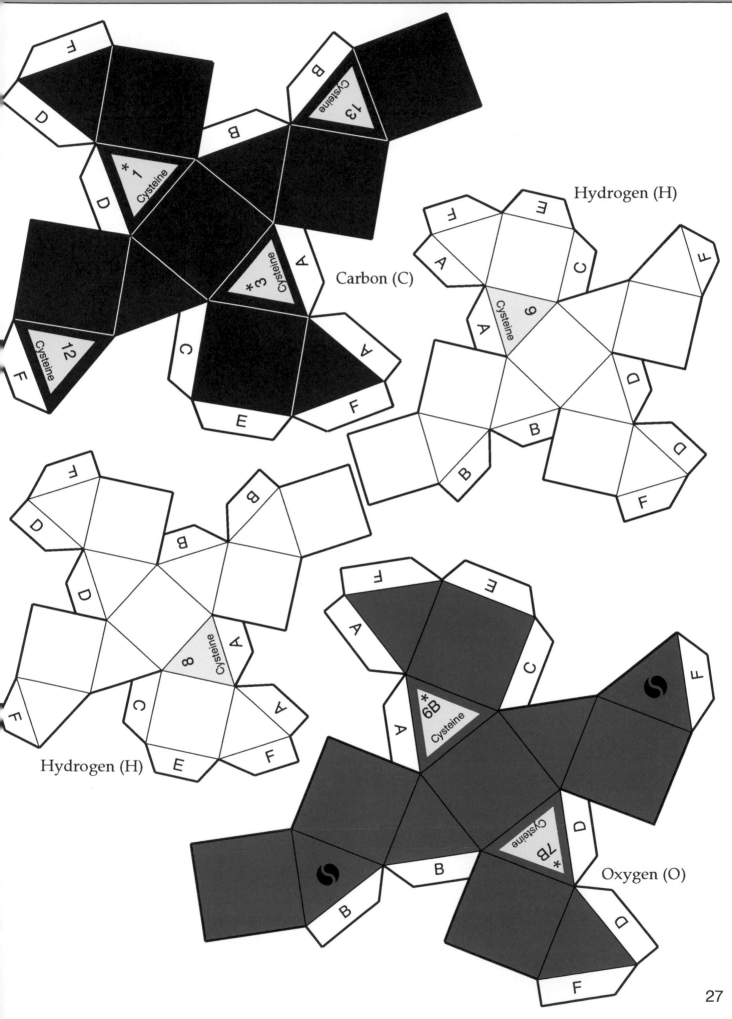

Carbon (C)

Hydrogen (H)

Hydrogen (H)

Oxygen (O)

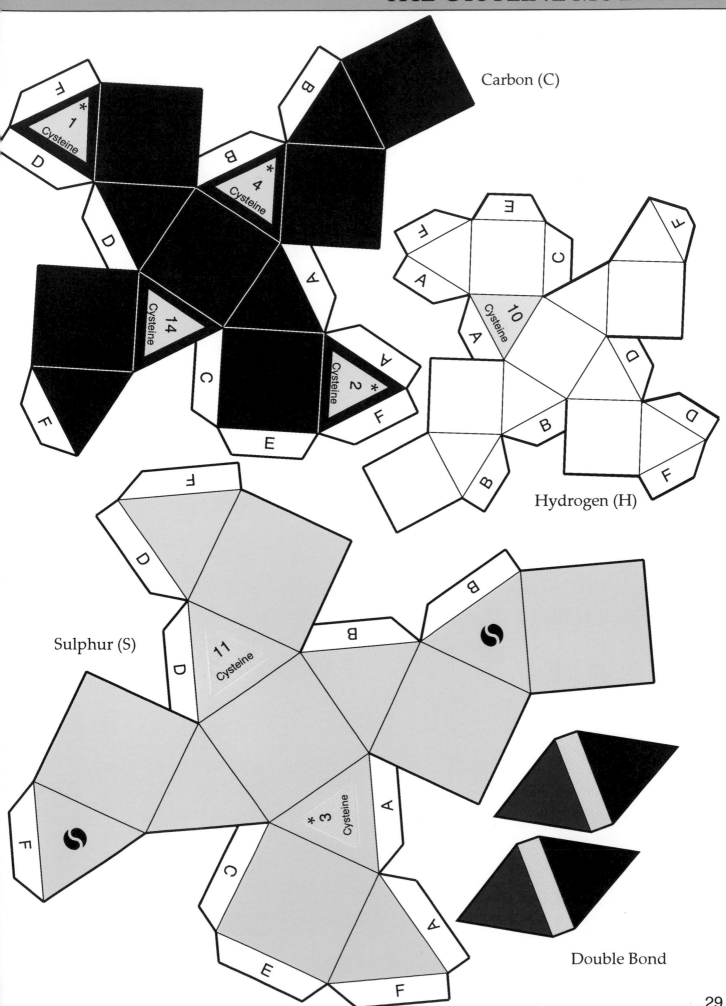

Carbon (C)

Hydrogen (H)

Sulphur (S)

Double Bond

*7A

Cysteine

Cysteine

7B*

*6A

Cysteine

Cysteine

6B*

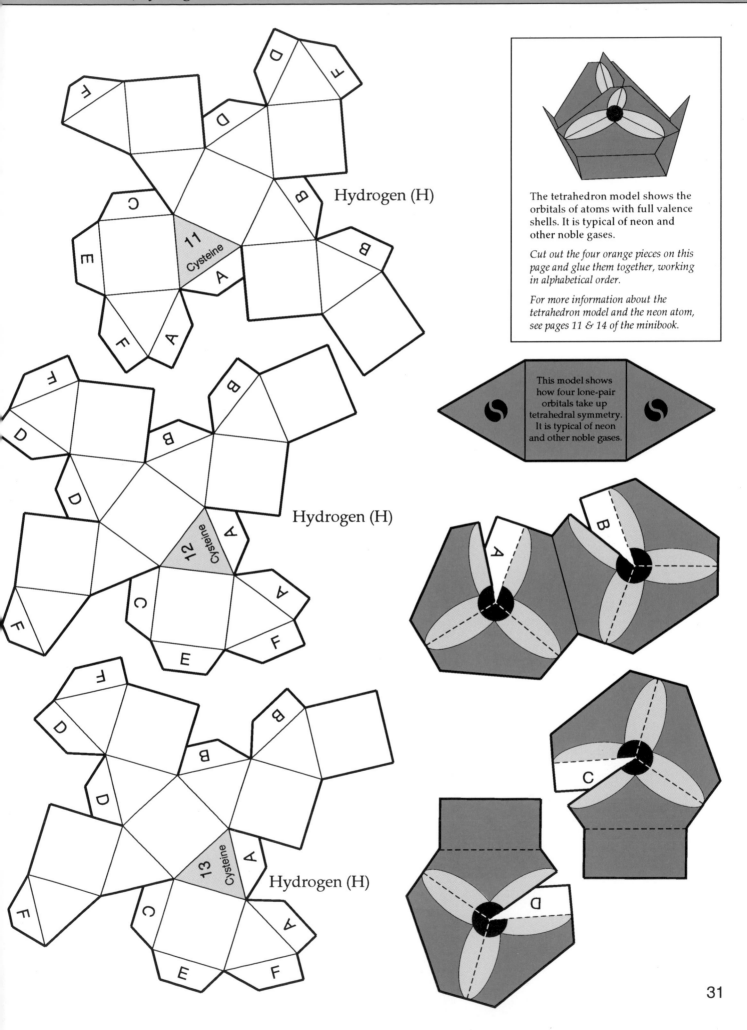

Hydrogen (H)

11
Cysteine

Hydrogen (H)

12
Cysteine

Hydrogen (H)

13
Cysteine

The tetrahedron model shows the orbitals of atoms with full valence shells. It is typical of neon and other noble gases.

Cut out the four orange pieces on this page and glue them together, working in alphabetical order.

For more information about the tetrahedron model and the neon atom, see pages 11 & 14 of the minibook.

This model shows how four lone-pair orbitals take up tetrahedral symmetry. It is typical of neon and other noble gases.